Send Our Reps to Rehab

PRESTON PICUS

Published by Pragmatic Publishing

Cover Art by Eli Ehlinger

Cover Design by Erickson Foster

ISBN: 0615759203
ISBN-13: 978-0615759203

DEDICATION

For my people.

SEND OUR REPS TO REHAB

CONTENTS

SEND OUR REPS TO REHAB

SEND OUR REPS TO REHAB

1 STOP WORRYING AND FIGHT

I have been pissed, man. Really pissed.

I'm watching the news on TV and the way these actors pretending to be journalists say crazy things to get people going. Then I'm watching the way our average Americans engage, rooting for political teams based on the crazy things the pretend journalists said on TV.

I'm watching elected officials selling us all down the river, taking in huge bribes that they call 'campaign donations' or 'lobbying' and smiling and waving and saying "Oh buddy boy, I'm a public servant! (wink wink, nod-nod)." I'm watching the Supreme Court say that there's nothing wrong with being bribed. I'm watching the President brag about how many big bribes he's gotten.

When did bribery become so acceptable? I wanted to know so I started reading books, tons of books, articles, reports, headlines, inside-jobs and outside opinions and everyone keeps saying how much they hate our representatives. Nothing about bribery, though, just a general dislike for the folks that we call 'Politicians.'

"They're assholes and crooks!"

So I say: Don't vote for them.

Somehow everyone disagrees with me.

"Oh, but I have to vote for one of the two teams so I just vote for the one that I hate the least."

"What else can you do?" people ask me. "If I don't vote for the least detestable of the two then my team might not win!"

What else can you do? This is always the question accompanied by a shrug.

Well I think it's time to do something.

I think it's time to fight.

Let's put the first thing first: Unless you give your Congressman more than $1,000 he doesn't know who you are.

Unless you give your Congresswoman $5,000 she's just pretending to care about you.

Unless you can throw some serious money into the system: It's not your system, no matter what the constitution says.

Some representatives say it's not their fault – the system is corrupted and they HAVE to get the money, you see. "When I go a-running for Congress I mean to do well, but I have to get some money if I'm going to get elected and the average American just doesn't have enough dough to keep me going. I need more. I have to take the really big bribes or else I can't get elected to office and do the good work."

They sound like addicts to me. Addicted to money. Addicted to bribes.

Addicts are known to make terrible decisions, and our money-addled reps make terrible choices every day.

We suppose they are trying to be public servants but which one of them is making the best choices for the public? Which one of them is in it for the people? Is your Rep of the people? Do you know how many bribes your Congressman or Congresswoman has taken?

Did your Rep turn down the big bribe/campaign donation? Which one of them refuses to skirt the issue and calls out the rest of them on the floor? Which one of them do you trust, personally?

Have you ever drank a beer with your Rep?

Have you ever been invited over to their house or had a Congresswoman say happy birthday to your kid or gone and partied with a Senator on someone's yacht?

No? Then I've got bad news friend: This is not your government.

Worse – you want worse? We watch them partying with their rich friends, we watch the bribes go down and we do nothing.

Remember the weeklong Conventions?

The Democratic Party holds a Convention to pat themselves on the back and party with the millionaires that give them those wonderful campaign bribes and we watch on TV. The Republican Party does the same thing, same speeches about how it's time to look out for regular Americans, the middle class they say, it's time to make America work again and then they party all night on Goldman Sachs' corporate yacht.

We watch them like jealous girlfriends who thought they were in love with us.

What can we do? We're always saying that: What can we do?

We can stop it. We can, oh believe me. This is still America and we're still a democracy and the OG's that signed those papers two hundred and forty years ago got some things right. It's our country still and we can stand up.

As I say: It's time to fight.

But we have to fight smart.

I've been wanting to get into it for quite some time but I've noticed that Congress has a long history of not listening to regular folks. Mark Twain hated Congressmen in the late 1800's and Warren Harding sold Americans down the river worse than Bush Jr or Obama could dream just before the Great Depression.

It takes some time to find the thread: Where can we start this fight and have impact and make some changes?

You see, we have a few problems in this country: The middle class is getting shafted but the news networks won't tell the story. The wealthy interests are winning, big time, in a way that is unhealthy for our American way of life. Our people are fatter, less informed, and less optimistic about the future than they have ever been. There are many fortunes to be made fostering this despair. Another amoral millionaire stars in his own new reality TV show every day while we reduce the salaries of teachers and social workers.

In addition: We have the worst leadership which our nation has ever suffered at a time when our citizens face the worst prospects in our history. Our elected representative leadership has turned its back on the majority of Americans just when we need them most. It's time to vote them out. It's time to get ourselves new Congressmen.

The first thing we have to do is something which is uncomfortable.

If you are among the huge majority of Americans, if you're among the 70% that thinks this government is run for a few special interests rather than the benefit of the Average American it is likely that you aren't enamored with the party you vote for. You vote for the Republicans or Democrats because you think they're better than the lousy other party, but you don't love any of them.

You think abortion is important, or immigration. Gun control gets you going or tax policy. Something pushes you, maybe it's welfare spending, and you say to yourself "Shit, both of these choices suck but I'm going to vote for this important thing. I'm going to vote for whichever one of these two liars is going to go my way on this issue."

And that's fine. We're all uninspired. We've all done it.

Abortion, immigration, gun control, unemployment, health care…

These are complex issues.

But if we are going to fix this country then we need to look at the bigger picture.

If we are going to get our Congress back we have to make one issue more important than the rest of them. Just for a while.

We have to vote for candidates who are stopping the bribes. We have to vote for people who are really going to go in there and change the way we finance campaigns. The 70% of us who are rational and want a better America have to override the 30% who are either too selfish or too ignorant to see the crash course we are on and we Have To vote for the folks who are ethically financing their campaigns and not vote for the folks who are taking the big bribes called campaign donations.

So who are we going to vote for? Where are the candidates that don't take the bribes?

They're around, but you don't hear about them in the news or on TV.

These honest Americans who want to fight to stop the madness don't take the bribes. Because they don't take the bribes they don't have the money to spend buying commercials. CNN and FOX and MSNBC ignore them because CNN and FOX and MSNBC are in on the deal. They like the bribery system. They like owning a part of the Congress.

You have to go out and look for these candidates. They're there. They're going to get louder. But you have to find them, and vote for them. Even if they might disagree with you on one of those other issues.

Just for now.

Make your Rep swear that they'll put in the time to stop the corruption. Make them promise that they won't take any of the bribes themselves. And if they break the promise: Vote for somebody else.

We've got to stop letting these corrupt, greedy bastards hold us hostage with our own values.

We've got to send a message: If you take bribes we don't want you in Congress.

End of story.

2 THE SYSTEM IS DESIGNED FOR TROUBLE

> "People who contribute get the ear of the member and the ear of the staff. They have access – and access is it. Access is power."
> Romano Mazzoli (D-Kentucky)
> *Quoted in* Republic, Lost *by Lawrence Lessig*

The problem starts with how our officials get into office.

They have to buy their way in every two years.

It costs about $1.3million to run for Congress. The job only pays $175,000 a year. The job costs more than seven times what it pays.

Our elected officials don't always have more than a million dollars laying around to throw into a campaign. So they do fundraising.

Currently you can give $5,000 to a candidate for Congress or a Congresswoman and it's not bribery.

It's a campaign donation.

Currently you can open up a Super Pac and spend as much money as you want on a candidate for Congress and it's totally legal.

It's free speech.

Who's speaking?

0.26% of Americans donate more than $200.

99.74% of Americans are using less than $200 of their available free speech.

Perhaps some people just have more free speech laying around than others.

0.05% of Americans put up 90% of the money for the elections.

That's 5 out of every 10,000.

If you're ever at a football game with 80,000 screaming fans – odds are that one short row of them matter to our elected officials.

This means that the other 99.95% of Americans are merely 'voters.'

Think about it: When you vote once every couple of years you choose between a few candidates on the ballot. It's been set, you can now decide between the folks who made it.

But how did they get there?

Turns out that before you even think about checking that box thousands of little decisions have already been made. Dozens of potential candidates in your area have been eliminated. You had no input. You were waiting for the chance to vote.

While you were waiting for Election Day the 0.05% of Americans who are financing our elections have gone through the trouble of deciding who is a 'viable' candidate. This small group of investors choose the choices.

Sure, you can pick between the two or three they've agreed upon, but is this how democracy should work?

The important thing to understand is that large campaign contributions are nothing more than Bribes. Giving a Congressman or several Congresswomen $5,000 apiece should be illegal. It's not, but it should be.

Because our officials are forced to get the money in order to run this results in what we call a Baptism by Bribery. The only thing our Congressmen all have in common is that they've gotten their hands on a lot of money.

It's the test any idealistic woman or man considering a run for office must first pass.

It's the first thing we ask: Can you get the money?

If you can, then you will be considered. If you cannot: Our system doesn't care what your ideas are, or how you plan to work in Congress. If you cannot get the money then you cannot be in Congress or the Senate. You cannot be President.

And so politicians begin the process of accumulating cash. If they have the money already – fine. They spend their own wealth to obtain the position. Perhaps we can see that it is slightly unfair that a wealthy businessman or a successful attorney can run for office while a talented teacher or a dedicated researcher has to find the cash. Maybe that's not the best thing for the country.

However it is even worse in instances where the candidate must reach out to willing donors for their money as his or her lifeblood in the campaign cycle. This makes our Congressmen and Congresswomen Dependent Upon Their Donors, leaves them Begging for Bribes.

Like junkies committing crimes for the next fix - Our Reps Will Do

Anything To Get That Money.

Now you might begin to wonder: What exactly is it that they are doing in return for all that dough?

It starts slowly: First they let wealthy interests touch them.

If you've got money to spend, these candidates will have dinner with you, invite you to their office, fly on your jet, go for a weekend at the beach or skiing or out dancing at the nightclubs with you.

If you've got the cash to spend you can party with our candidates at the Conventions, you can hold hands on stage, you can Facetime with them on your iPhones.

What about the rest of us? Aren't we good Americans? Why don't I get to go dancing with Nancy Pelosi? Why don't I get to play on a yacht with John Boehner?

Because I didn't give them any money.

Did you?

Once this tiny group is touching our representatives the cuddling goes to the next level: They develop a relationship.

Soon they're more than just friends, they're doing birthdays and holidays. The donors are visiting our Congressmen at the office. Sometimes they're just shooting the shit, but sometimes they're talking about pieces of legislation.

Yes, when these special money givers are hanging around with our Reps decisions are being made about the future of our country. There is a table with a limited number of seats: The more money you give the better chance you have of being in the room while important discussions take place. Money is appropriated, laws are enacted, policy is set and not one of us regular, middle-income Americans is in there.

We didn't give them enough money. Nobody is at the table Representing Us.

Then they come back and tell us how it's all going to work. We can say "Well I don't think that's a good idea!" But we are talking to our TV's, wishing we could talk to our Reps.

You try to email your Congresswoman. She sends you an email thanking you for taking the time to email her. You email again, she sends the same thankful email back.

You email your Senator. He sends you an identical email thanking you for taking the time.

"I don't want you to pass that goddamn law!" you scream. But they can't hear you. You didn't give them $5,000. You don't have $5,000 to give anyway. You certainly don't have the money to start a Super Pac to funnel campaign finance bribes to your favorite candidates or the resources to hire an expensive lobbyist. You're not a millionaire, unfortunately.

Our representatives go back to their committees with some directions their funders have given them and soon some money is going in a new direction. Pretty soon some new laws are passed and there's some pork in there that you have to dig and research to find out about.

You're pissed: It's your country, this person is supposed to represent you but he doesn't give a shit what you say.

Then it comes time to vote, but you're afraid that the other team will win so you vote for her anyway. She didn't listen to you, she didn't think about you when she was making her decisions, she took bribes and you know it but you vote for her again anyway.

They know that you're going to vote for them no matter what, just so long as they can get the money.

There's a great book called Winner Take All Politics by these economists Jacob S. Hacker and Paul Pierson which shows exactly how dangerous this is for you and me, for the third wheel in this cozy little coterie.

It turns out that the wealthy few are getting a helluva lot more for their money than we bargained for.

It goes like this:

In the 1970's campaign costs started to go up. In 1974 the average congressional campaign cost $54,000. In 2008 the price had jumped up to $1,300,000.

That's a 2,400% increase.

A car which cost $10,000 in 1974 would have to cost $240,000 in 2008 to make the same jump.

Nobody would pay $240,000 for a van. Why would anybody pay $1.3million for an election?

The reasons for this change are varied, however the effect of this increase is the most important aspect affecting our national government. Congresswomen have to get the money. They are addicted to dough. They will do whatever it takes.

And worse: You won't think they are serious candidates until they do.

Investors see it another way: The US Government spends more than $3,000,000,000,000 ($3trillion) every year.

The return on investment in DC is incredible: For every dollar you spend lobbying or bribing Congressmen you get $220 back. That's a 22,000% return. Those are INCREDIBLE profits.

You would be a fool NOT to invest in some bribery on Capitol Hill if you get the chance. Your company would have to be stupid not to take advantage of this loophole.

But if you're not getting big money from the bribes our elected officials are taking: You would be equally idiotic to let it keep happening.

That's why some of us think it's time to fight.

3 THE GREAT BARRIER

Here's the truth: They think you're stupid, that you won't bother to check up on what's going on behind the scenes. They think that you're going to keep voting for one of these two political teams because there's nothing else you can do.

And they're right…right?

You aren't going to go out looking for a real Representative, you aren't going to go out and donate your small money to a person that will likely lose, you aren't going to go out and find change – you're going to take the less repulsive of the two options 0.05% of America has picked out for you.

You're going to say that immigration or gun control or abortion or gay rights is more important to you than a government which is responsive to the needs of the people.

You're going to say that it's more important that your team wins than it is for your Representative to look out for your best interests.

You're going to say that you already know that politicians are corrupt, that they've always been corrupt and there's nothing you can do to stop it anyway.

You're going to forget any of this is going on in a week.

Right?

I say wrong.

I say it's time to find some real candidates. They're out there. You can Google them in whatever district you reside. You can dig and find somebody that isn't taking the big bribes. You'll have to dig hard because they're not a serious candidate until they take some money.

You have to dig hard because 'everybody' believes that not voting for a Democrat or Republican is a waste of your vote.

After you start to support a clean candidate you can support legislation which puts people ahead of money again, which stops campaign donations from ruling our legislators. Often it's called Campaign Finance Reform but you have to be careful. Sometimes the tricky lobbyists make laws that reform campaign finance to make it *easier* to bribe our officials.

You can demand that your Rep get off the money, that she kicks the habit and swears to stop taking these bribes. You can threaten him with his job. You can threaten them with your vote.

You can ignore the crazy shit they're saying on TV. You can stop being afraid that every month is another fiscal cliff. You can say something like "If you threaten me with one more crisis that you yourselves have invented I am going to vote for ANYBODY that is not you."

Because the reality is this: We won't get the solution we want for anything that's important to us as long as our Congress is not dependent upon us, the American People.

We won't get anything we need, we won't have the government we deserve as long our Representatives don't have to listen to US. To the People.

It's time to stop the bribery.

It's time to fight.

4 WHAT IS AT STAKE?

We are facing economic crisis. We are facing a potentially destabilized United States. Why?

History tells us that when there is a disparity in wealth so that the top 0.1% is taking home too much of the dough then the middle class gets squeezed and things begin to fall apart. It's basic economics: It is best for our country when the middle class gets a fair share of the growth and wealth.

Now, wealthy interests have been squeezing the middle class since before we invented money and so it's natural, in a way, for these corporations and millionaires and unions to try to take bigger and bigger pieces of the pie.

But you can see in history that when the middle class gets squeezed too much you have destabilization followed by crises and then rebellion and revolution. This is what happened in Russia and France and even Spain to an extent when those countries turned themselves upside down.

It's no good for the country. It's better if you can make change without all that.

We have to fight before it gets ugly. We have to defend our position before we're defending our homes and our livelihood.

5 SOME TECHNICAL DETAILS

"Liberal democracy requires an awkward balance between two spheres of life. Within the sphere of democratic politics, we confront each other as moral equals, and we deliberate about our collective future. It is not good enough to say 'I want it!' We must make a good-faith effort to justify public decisions as serving the public good. This is what responsible citizenship is all about.

"The organizing principles of a liberal market are different. We come to the table with unequal assets, often vastly unequal. We bargain to further our private interest without trying to justify our deals in terms of the greater public interest. It is good enough to say 'I want it!': That's what freedom is all about.

"These two spheres are equal parts of the American way of life and inasmuch they remain opposites and equals to one another. The liberal market drives creativity and productivity while democratic equality ensures the rights and freedoms of each citizen shall not be trampled underfoot.

"If we are to accept that democratic equality can check market inequality in a way which legitimizes the economic outcomes, then we cannot allow market inequalities to have an overwhelming impact on these deliberations. If this happens, we can no longer say that we, as citizens, have authorized the pervasive inequalities we experience as market actors. Politics will have been transformed into a forum in which big money praises itself."

-Argument by Ackerman and Ayers in *Voting With Dollars*

I have been reading about campaign finance for the last 18 months – more than 50 books, hundreds of journal articles, conversations with experts, round table discussions, political theory…the works.

Campaign finance and the reform of our system is perhaps the most complicated subject which I have found to study. In some ways it's more complicated than quantum mechanics and the tricky relationships we find in physics.

Campaign finance is difficult to consider because it falls in the region between the two main pillars of American society: Our equal democracy and our free market.

Our free market is a place of competition and inequality and we say that this is good. Each person brings their own levels of talent and wealth to the table and competes for success. This is the basis of capitalism.

Our equal democracy, on the other hand, is supposed to be a place of total parity and we say that this is good as well. All men and women are created equal before the American government; equal justice, equal voting rights, equal treatment under the law – our government is supposed to treat each American as an American and that is that.

In our equal democracy it should not matter if you are a millionaire or a minimum wage laborer – one person, one vote.

Campaign finance is where these two foundations of the United States meet, where these spheres touch. Candidates must run campaigns. Campaigns are going to cost money. This is certain. The question is this: How can we ensure that the cost of campaigns and the effort to obtain that money does not destroy our political process? How can we provide for campaigns to be funded without ruining the equal democracy?

How much money can powerful players in the free market spend influencing the decisions of the democratic process before it is too much?

It is obvious that the amount being spent now is too much. In this case: What should we do?

Unlike many other scholars, I argue that there is no silver bullet to solve this incredibly complex issue. My solution is as complex and as 'messy' as the situation itself.

It seems to me that changing the way our political process works is dependent upon people changing their assumptions about the value of particular issues. The solution is big: Start by looking for the candidates that don't take the bribes. Follow the lead of the groups who are doing very good fighting: Rootstrikers, Common Cause, Democracy Matters, etc. Do research on maplight.org which is a non-partisan data machine connecting the money to the officials.

Or look for someone you trust to do some of this leg work for you and when the time comes commit to the good laws, the good candidates, the good anti-bribery action.

You may have to forgo voting for your team for a couple of elections but in the end it will be worth it.

6 WHAT'S HAPPENING NOW

According to Lawrence Lessig:

70% of American voters said they could trust the government in Washington in 1980. However, only 22% of American voters said they could trust the government in Washington almost always or most of the time in 2010.

In 1964 – 64% of Americans thought the government was run for the benefit of all. 29% for the benefit of a few special interests.

In 2008 – 29% of Americans thought the government was run for the benefit of all. 69% for the benefit of a few special interests.

What has changed?

In 1974 the average cost of running for congress was $54,000. In 2008 the average campaign cost $1,300,000.

Television advertising, internet, billboards, fliers and information dissemination generally has overflowed beyond the traditional boundaries. In response to this campaigns have pushed into the expanding fields.

In addition, the new 24 hour news media cycles are available for constant agenda and propaganda pushing; Like commentators at a football game, political pundits and pretend journalists need something to say. These talking points are provided by the ceaseless campaigning infused with the new money and pushed by the new mediums of communication.

This process continues until we have a clearly limitless campaign season in which candidates promote themselves for market shares in the same way Coke battles Pepsi – with no boundaries, with no pauses, with no reflection.

However: You must do this to win. One cannot stand aside and claim the moral high ground – that is election suicide.

The biggest trouble with what's happening now is this: By allowing the wealthiest to purchase our elections we are destroying the legitimacy of our own social fabric. American democracy, a free and equal democracy, is the thing which separates us from lower forms of government. The equal democracy legitimizes the free market. An equal democracy is the cornerstone of our civilization – and we have lost it.

Our current government is unresponsive to the people – it is deadened to the will of the majority of citizens through the purchase of candidates which takes place during the never-ending election cycles.

I'm not saying that the wealthy interests purchasing our elected officials have it in for the average American, that they are somehow 'out to get us.'

It's merely that the Average American is not represented at the table where deals are being made. You have to donate at least $1,000 to get a short conversation with your Congressman or Congresswoman. You must donate $5,000 every two years to be taken at all seriously. And to be on the 'in'? Bundle 10 friends who donate $5,000 apiece or funnel money through your Super Pac and bribe dozens of elected officials. That is access, that is power and that is it.

And we don't have it.

Increasingly Americans view the system as corrupt, as inept, as without value. This makes the big wins by the big winners in the free market harder to stomach. With no sense of fair hearing or of equality in our democracy the free market seems a sham.

We all lose when a rabid, amoral government attacks citizens with felonies for relatively minor crimes while ignoring the lawlessness and depravity of the banking institutions which collapsed our economy.

Additionally, many studies have shown that over the last 30 years the gap between the wealthiest few and the Average American has expanded. While the overall wealth of the United States has grown, only the top 1%, and really the top 0.1%, have seen the full benefits of this growth.

You, as an Average American, have not enjoyed the benefit of our country's success.

For instance: If you make $30,000 a year and had the last 30 years of growth been shared equally and not distributed to the top 0.1%, then you would be making closer to $40,000 now.

If you make $60,000 you should be at $72,000.

If you make $100,000 you should be around $118,000.

However if you make $1,000,000 you should be making more like $870,000. If you make $5,000,000 you should be seeing something more like $3,900,000. And if you make more than $10,000,000 your income around $7,300,000.

This isn't wealth redistribution. This is about more Americans seeing the benefit of our nation's financial growth. This is about getting our fair share of the profits.

But because our equal democracy is being leveraged by the big winners in our free market and we have a government which is purchased by the wealthiest few, the most powerful device in our equal democracy is doing its best to reward those who spend their time bribing our officials with an increasingly large piece of the pie.

Turn this tide, vote out the corrupted officials who are taking these bribes: Your salary will go up.

You will feel more comfortable. You will make more money.

Sure, the wealthy few are going to refute this. They will spend a few million to hire some corrupted economists to tell you crazy things.

"If an executive making $5,000,000 is suddenly only making $3,900,000 she is NOT going to be as creative. She won't make as many jobs!"

But this is foolish.

Where that one 'innovator' makes an extra $1.1million we could see 110 mid-level workers make an additional $10,000. Can anyone disinterestedly argue that one person making millions and getting a million more is going to work harder than one hundred and ten people making $40,000 and getting a 25% increase in pay?

In other words: How much more would a $40k/year worker do to be a $50k/year worker? How much would 100 $40k/year workers do to be $50k/year workers?

Isn't the answer A LOT? Isn't the answer A LOT more than one millionaire can do?

Of course, if you have the money, if you're super rich then you are immorally smart to play this game, right? I mean, it's terrible to do. It's greedy, it's foolish, it is breaking our country but you don't get to the top of the corporate ladder by caring about other people's needs.

Of course the math says hire the economist, threaten to ship jobs overseas, wrangle the officials you've bribed, spend $10,000,000 to save $50,000,000 but whatever you do don't give up the edge you've got.

However We the People must be self-interested as well. We must demand a government which responds to our needs, to US, the Average Americans who live in the middle of this great nation. The body must for once respond to the backbone and the muscles and the skin and forget the sweetness receptor on the tongue for the sake of its own survival.

It's how democracy is supposed to work, and when our democracy begins to work this way again we will see a decrease in instability, an increase in prosperity and a better America for our children.

We must act in self-interest, and our self-interest as the rational, intelligent, hard working 70% of Americans is this: Vote for candidates who won't take the bribes.

7 CONCLUSION

We live in a critical age in the history of our great nation. Separated from the intelligence and integrity of our forefathers by two and a half centuries we look to gain a new foothold in the coming ages of technology and rapid globalization.

Our species has learned new things in this last century that could not have been predicted by the previous generations. Our traditions are steeped in the brilliance and power of those who have gone before but our future depends on our ability to use the new and powerful information which we are discovering to create modern interpretations of our systems of economics and governance.

I do not yet have any serious recommendations beyond fixing what I consider to be the single most obvious problem facing our population: Our elected officials are owned, outright, by a tiny fraction of Americans and respond very well to this very small group while responding not very well to the majority of my countrymen and women.

If we can change the way campaigns are financed in a meaningful way which does not trample the First Amendment but does not allow the excessive abuses which we currently suffer then we will have done something to move our country in the right direction.

There are incredibly smart, incredibly strong people in this great nation but for some reason I see very few of them running for office. Perhaps it is the corruptive nature of selling yourself, perhaps it is the monotony and inglorious drudgery of steeping yourself in the pride-swallowing self-abasement known as the political game. Maybe scientists and researchers and doctors and engineers and teachers and creative geniuses simply find it absurd and refuse to put themselves through the nastiness of the process by which one gains power.

Perhaps the system is tilted toward actors, lawyers and schmoozers.

Whatever the reasons we must find a way to attract higher level candidates to the job of running our country. My next pamphlet will deal with some of these issues and offer some new ideas toward this end.

However let me say quickly here what I have been thinking for some time: It has been more than 100 years since the discovery of Relativity. It has been more than 80 years since we discovered some incredibly interesting things about the nature of atomic and sub-atomic particles which we call Quantum Mechanics. During this time the world shrank as we began driving cars, then riding in airplanes in ever increasing numbers. We ship goods to one another around the world at a massive rate which defies traditional forms of thinking. We carry more information in our pocket than is in any set of encyclopedias.

It is time, in my opinion, that we rethink some of these very old ideas to which we cling. I enjoy Adam Smith and John Maynard Keynes, but it is important to remember these individuals lived and wrote quite some time ago. There are powerful strengths in our accepted forms of economics, however there are equally powerful weaknesses which have not yet been overcome and our philosophy has stagnated under the pressure of constant interpretation of what was said in the past.

It is time, in my opinion, that we develop a new system of socio-economic and political interaction which takes into account this new and emerging world in which we find ourselves. I very much admire Albert Einstein who is noted as much for his brilliance as his daring. When he pushed the physics world with his four papers in 1905 it was as much fearlessness as it was intelligence which allowed him to discover new and important things about the universe. He was not afraid to defy the traditional wisdom of his contemporaries.

This is what we need in our elected officials: We need them to be daring.

But not in the way which we have come to expect – that they will occasionally say something insane or stupid or designed to infuriate the voters who are not on their political team.

We need them to be daring in a new and positive way which helps move our country forward at a time when many of us are feeling despair and anguish regarding our endlessly insipid state of governance.

Perhaps it is the case that the folks we have in office cannot do this. Perhaps we have elected too many duds and the process is gummed up.

Fine. Let us find new and creative and daring leaders to take control of this beautiful ship, to steer us fearlessly into the future.

Let us not be consumed by what has been said or what has happened already. Let us expect more. Let us demand better. Let us fight. Let us fight a little bit every day and let us win small battles every year.

Let us take our country back, piece by piece if we must, before it is too late.

8 FURTHER READING

Republic, Lost – Lawrence Lessig
Winner Take All Politics – Hacker and Pierson
Voting With Dollars – Ayers and Ackerman
So Damn Much Money – Robert G. Kaiser
The Value of Nothing – Raj Patel
Life Without Lawyers – Philip K Howard
Culture of Narcissism – Christopher Lasch
Love and Will – Rollo May
Philosophy and Physics – Werner Heisenberg
The World as I See It – Albert Einstein
The Lonely Crowd – David Riesman
The Power Elite – C. Wright Mills
Amusing Ourselves to Death – Neil Postman
The Rebel – Albert Camus
Candide – Voltaire

Catch up with Preston at www.fouras.org
Email: info@fouras.org

Made in the USA
Monee, IL
04 November 2026

67382730R00017